Jambo, Rafiki
"hello, my friend"

STORIES FOR CHILDREN

BY

Figen Gündüz Letaconnoux
(Afrigo)

UNITED STATES OF AMERICA
Copyright© 2016

Published by
Cosmo Publishing Company - USA
&
Yazardan Direkt - Turkey

Cover & Layout by
Victoria Johnson

Turkish to English Translation by
Cağla Miniç

All rights reserved, including the rights of reproduction in whole or in part in any form

ISBN: 978-605-83475-1-9

Once upon a time, far, far away in the land of Africa, there were vast forests with huge lakes, long rivers, endless lowlands, supreme mountains and high rocks. And in those forests there were cute Baboons, angry Rhinos, long-necked Giraffes, Ox-Headed Antelopes, cheerful Goats, spotted Leopards, Warthogs with vertical tails, Zebras in striped pajamas, and countless animals all living happily together.

Local stories about these cute animals have been told for generations, and I have gathered them to share with children of all ages to teach them priceless lessons.

I also spent ten years in Africa with our animal friends, taking pictures, learning, as well as writing stories of them.

I hope children will enjoy reading and learning about our animal friends, and take valuable lessons from these local African stories to better our world.

Afrigo!

A FEW WORDS IN SWAHILI (ALSO KNOWN AS KISWAHILI)

Antelope - *Palahala*
Elephant - *Tembo*
Baboon - *Nyani*
Leopard - *Chui*
Warthodg - *Ngiri*
Goat - *Mbuzi*
Rhino - *Kifaru*
Giraffe - *Twiga*
Crocodile - *Mamba*
Aardvark - *Mhanga*
Zebra - *Pundamilia*
Snake - *Nyoka*

Hi, Hello - *Jambo*
Bye Bye - *Kwa Kheri*
Not a Problem, All Good - *Hakuna Matata*
Thank You - *Asante Sana*
Welcome - *Karibu, Karibuni* (plural)
Friend - *Rafiki*
Child - *Mtoto*
Sky - *Ubinguni*
How Are You - *Habari Gani?*

Fun Fact: Swahili is a combination of Arabic and some of the local African dialects. There are 80 million people in East Africa who currently speak Swahili.

WHY ARE GIRAFFE'S NECK AND LEGS LONG?
Local East African Folktale

Once upon a time, on the coast of the Indian Ocean in East Africa, there lived Giraffe. Giraffe didn't always have long legs and a long neck. In fact his neck was short and stubby, like Rhino's.

At that time the sun dried out the water wells and lakes and made the grass tasteless and not so green. Because of this our animal friends were looking for a solution to their hunger and thirst problems.

One day, when Giraffe was looking for tasty grass, he came across his friend Rhino…

"Grass is so tasteless now… I miss the fresh, green and tasty grass that we used to eat after the rain," said Giraffe.

Rhino pulled out a tuft of dry grass with his strong mouth and said, "You're right my friend, I miss it too. I can hardly eat this dry, tasteless grass. It's been a long time since the last rain; we all are missing that fresh, green, tasty grass."

"A loooong time" said Giraffe, nodding his head. Giraffe looked around and said, "other animals ate all the grass and there is nothing left for us. I would love to eat the fresh leaves on the top of these trees."

"But we can't reach up there," said Rhino. Suddenly his eyes twinkled with joy. "I have a plan…we can find a Human friend and ask him for his help!" He cried with excitement.

Giraffe and Rhino went on a long walk to find a Human friend. They went up a hill and down a dale, ate dry grass when they were hungry and drank the little water that they could find.

They were getting really, really tired when they came across a Human. They explained their problem under the shade of an Acacia tree and waited to hear his answer.

"I think I might be able to help you. Come back here tomorrow at noon. I am going to give you a plant, and you'll be surprised to see what happens when you eat it," said the Human. Giraffe and Rhino agreed to come back the next day as they walked away in different directions.

Rhino was still hungry, and thinking to find green and tasty grass in the far far lands he decided to take a long journey.

Meanwhile, Giraffe decided to stay for another day.

The next morning, Giraffe and the Human met under the shining sun. As the Human was admiring Giraffe's skin with beautiful brown spots, he asked "Where is Rhino?"

"I don't know…we went in different directions after we talked to you yesterday and I haven't seen him since then," said Giraffe.

They waited for awhile but Rhino did not show. So the Human gave all the plants to Giraffe. He told him that the plants would make his neck and legs grow so he would be able to reach to the top of even the highest trees.

Giraffe ate the plants and watched his neck and legs grow. He was shocked by this extraordinary situation. He left the dry meadows and traveled far away where he could reach the highest branches of Acacia trees to eat the freshest, greenest, most tasteful leaves. This was a miracle!

Thanks to his long neck and legs, he stopped eating the dry grass on the ground, now able to reach the fresh and green leaves on the highest branches of trees. He was pleased and proud of his elegant neck.

It was almost sundown when Rhino came back. "Where are my plants?" He asked the Human with anger.

"You didn't show up on time this morning, so I gave it all to Giraffe. Haven't you noticed his long neck and legs?" Said the Human.

Rhino was very angry! He kicked the dust in front of him with his heavy, thick legs. He thought his friend Giraffe and the Human betrayed him.

Since that day, whenever Rhino sees a Human he gets angry and kicks the dust with his right foot.

INTERESTING FACTS ABOUT GIRAFFE
(Giraffa Camelopardalis)

- Giraffes are the world's tallest mammals.
- They can't lie down because of their height, so they sleep standing for a maximum of two hours a day.
- They have horns; male giraffe's horns are longer than females because male giraffes use them for protecting their families.
- Male giraffes can reach up to 16 feet, and females about 15 feet.
- They're herbivorous and generally eat leaves that other herbivores can't reach.
- They drink water every 5 days but can live without water for longer periods of time.
- They clean their nose, ears and eyes with their tongue which is almost 18 to 20 inches long.
- Thanks to their black, rough, sticky tongue they can eat even the thorns of the Acacia tree, one of the iconic symbols of Africa.
- They travel in small herds. Male giraffes leave their mothers and join single male friends when they are 3 years old.
- Their pregnancy lasts about 14-15 months. They give birth to one baby at a time. Mother giraffes breastfeed their babies for a year.

INTERESTING FACTS ABOUT RHINO
(Diceros Bicornis - black / Ceratotherium Simum - white)

- There are two types of rhinos; black and white.

- Their eyesight is weak, but they have an excellent sense of smell and hearing. They can hear even the lowest sounds by turning their ears 360 degrees.

- They bow their heads and breathe heavily while stamping their front feet, locking onto their targets to attack with their horns.

- Rhinos have two horns. The horns are made of a protein called keratin; the same protein in your hair and nails.

- The black rhino is more aggressive than the white rhino and lives alone.

- Since white rhinos are calm they're easier to hunt which is why they're on the endangered animals list.

- They can run up to 30 miles per hour in short distances.

- They live with parasite eating birds. Birds usually perch on the top of them and clean their skins by eating the parasites. Birds make a special sound when they eat the parasites to let the rhinos know.

- Rhino pregnancy lasts almost 18 months. They give birth to one baby at a time. Mother rhino breast feeds her baby for two years.

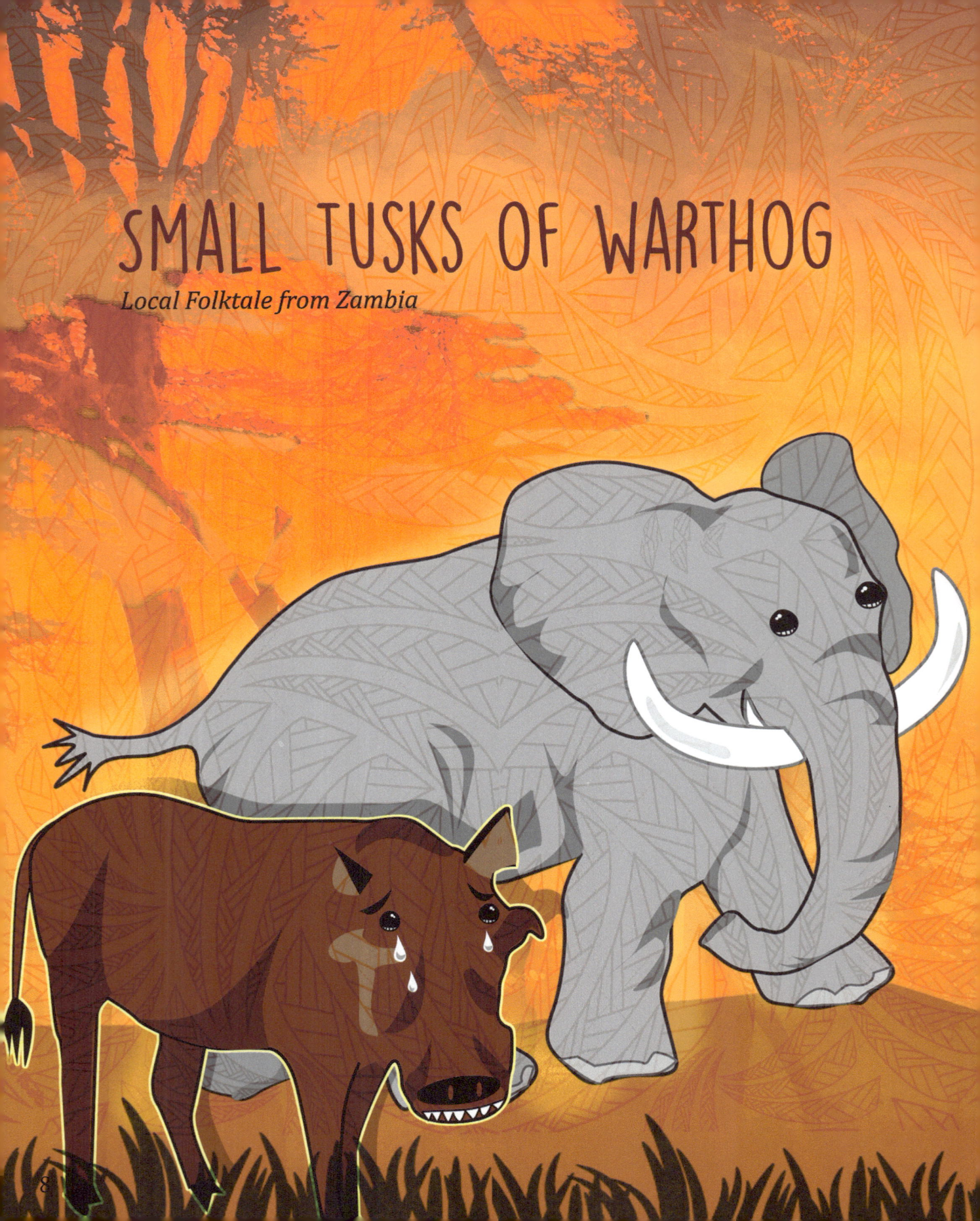

Once upon a time in Zambia, Elephant and his nephew Warthog were living together as a family. Warthog was a tiny copy of his uncle Elephant. Warthog had a small body with long curvy and glamorous teeth. Elephant had a huge body with small, not so glamorous teeth. Because of this, Elephant was a little ashamed but didn't want anybody to know it.

They wandered on the vast meadows, always together as best friends, sharing everything they found. In time, Elephant fell in love with the glamorous teeth of his best friend, Warthog. One day, Elephant saw Warthog trying to dig out the roots of a tree with his teeth…

Elephant said; "Hey, how would you like to exchange our teeth? Maybe we can use each other's teeth for awhile and return them at some date in the future."

Warthog was tired of carrying his heavy teeth. He thought he could take a rest for a while, so he accepted Elephant's offer. After the exchange, Warthog went back to the meadows and took long walks without getting tired.

In the meantime, Elephant was showing off his new teeth to all the animals in Africa. In fact, he was so happy with his long and glamorous teeth, he was not planning on returning them to Warthog at all.

GIRAFFE AND WARTHOG'S FRIENDSHIP

Figen Gündüz Letaconnoux

Warthog, who lost his tusks to Elephant, didn't know whom to believe or trust. By losing his long teeth, Warthog lost his self-confidence and wandered around the meadows for a long time…

Aardvark, who welcomed him into his home every night, was very wise and Warthog trusted Aardvark so much he started telling his story in good faith.

"Aardvark, every evening you welcome me into your home and make me feel safe. I owe you so much…thank you! However, during the day while eating my fair share, I want to feel secure just like in the evenings I'm with you…

You're the most hospitable, most good-hearted and the wisest of the pig family. Please, show me the way out," said Warthog.

Aardvark thought for a long time while caressing the side of his long, sensitive snout. "Tomorrow is another day, trust me! We'll find a way out of this," said Aardvark to Warthog.

In his dream that night, Aardvark had long talks with other animals of Africa about Warthog's safety during the day. Of course Elephant was not involved, he was just watched, guilty, from afar.

Next morning, Aardvark was whistling with joy while fixing breakfast. Warthog, who just woke up, joined him as he was rubbing his eyes. Aardvark's morning joy was a sign that Warthog's days would be happier from now on.

After breakfast, Aardvark and Warthog started looking for Giraffe among the tall Acacia trees. When they found Giraffe he asked, "Are you looking for me, my friends?"

Aardvark was breathless because of the Giraffe's beauty. Once he gathered himself, he said "Yes, we were looking for you, my friend. To make a long story short, everyone heard about what happened between my friend Warthog and his Uncle Elephant…
I am sure you
did too."

Giraffe nodded his head, to say that he did. Aardvark continued his words… "Warthog has been spending nights at my place, but he needs a friend to feel safer during the daytime. Since Warthog is short, he has a hard time seeing when danger is coming. What do you say about being Warthog's day friend since you are the tallest animal in the jungle?"

Giraffe thought for a second and said "If you, Aardvark, are the most hospitable animal in the forest, then I am the most warm-hearted one. From now on, Warthog shall feel safe with me!"

Since then, Warthog feels safer as he spends his days with his best friend Giraffe, and nights with Aardvark.

INTERESTING FACTS ABOUT WARTHOG

(Phacochoerus Africanus)

- They have button shaped warts on their faces.
- They can reach to tubers of the trees thanks to their tusks.
- They also use their tusks as protection from predators such as cheetahs, lions and leopards.
- They are herbivorous.
- They usually sleep in aardvark caves.
- They can easily spot predators thanks to the eyes on both sides of their foreheads.
- They have an excellent sense of smell and hearing.
- Since they're short they bend on their front knees to feed and roam with long-necked giraffe's to keep aware of dangers.
- They travel in families. When there's danger, adults raise their tails so the young warthogs can follow their parents.
- They have no sweat glands so cover themselves with mud to stay cool.
- Their pregnancy lasts about 5.5 months and they give birth to 2-4 babies at a time.

GLAMOROUS SPOTS ON LEOPARD'S FUR

African Folktale

A long, long time ago, Leopard was resting on a big tree branch looking towards the high hills of Africa. He was enjoying a nice, peaceful day with a light breeze, and watching the colorful birds fly playfully from one branch to another.

As he was gazing through the meadows, he noticed Giraffe with his long legs and his long neck reaching up to the tops of the trees. He was amazed with Giraffe's beautiful skin with glamorous brown leaf-shaped spots…and when he looked to the other side he saw the black and white zebras with their mesmerizing skins, each zebra having his own gorgeous design different than the other.

When he looked at his own fur he saw nothing but a boring yellowish color that looked like brown, dry grass; almost the same as the King of the Jungle. He didn't want to be same color as Lion. He was determined to be different…but how?

He jumped down off the tree and started walking around in the meadows wondering how he could get a glamorous coat like Giraffe or the zebras. After a short while he came across Snake coiled up in the shadows on the clay ground.

"I am very sick and nobody will take care of me" complained Snake. Leopard was not surprised at all and said "It's just because the other animal friends think you're going to bite them. That's why it's hard for them to come closer to take care of you…"

Snake was heartbroken and started crawling away…

When Leopard realized that Snake meant well, he thought to himself: 'You know, Snake is actually a nice animal. Maybe I should become friends with him!'

"Snake, wait for me! I'll take care of you until you feel better," said Leopard.

Snake was so happy and in return asked Leopard if there was anything he could do for him.

"You know, Giraffe is so beautiful with his patchy brown skin, and the zebras are so mesmerizing with their black and white stripes. My biggest wish is to have glamorous spots on my fur," said Leopard. "My dull colored fur has no glamour," he added sadly.

Snake was surprised and said, "I have a plan, my friend. Let me bite you, but don't worry! My poison won't hurt you. You'll feel itchy and have spots of rash on your fur, but shortly after your itchiness will go away and the spots will stay…then you'll be glamorous above all animals!"

Leopard was excited, but of course a little bit frightened. As Snake was crawling towards him, Leopard stared at him, trying to look brave. Suddenly Snake bit him without a warning!

Leopard became dizzy and fell to the ground. He stayed on the ground without a twitch. Then, all of a sudden regained his strength and jumped back up on his feet.

He looked at his fur and saw he was covered with glamorous spots. "I don't look like the King of the Jungle anymore! My fur is no longer straw-colored. I have glamorous spots now! Thank you my friend, I knew I could trust you!"

Since then, glamorous Leopard and Snake have shared a great friendship in the African forests.

16

INTERESTING FACTS ABOUT LEOPARD
(Panthera Pardus)

- They're the highest climbers in the "big cat" family.
- They're not very sociable; they live alone in brushwood and in rocky terrains.
- They're 7 times more powerful than a human and can carry prey 3.5 times their weight up into trees (so other animals won't steal them.)
- "Leopardus" means spotted lion in Latin.
- They have a strong neck, chest and a long tail.
- Male leopards weigh about 130 lbs.
- They're the most successful hunters in Africa.
- Their eyes are close to each other giving them the ability to calculate hunting distances more accurately, like binoculars.
- They're carnivores. They eat coyotes, storks and impalas.
- The female's pregnancy lasts about 3.5 months. They give birth to 2-3 babies at a time.
- A newborn leopard's fur is thicker and longer than an adult leopard. It is grey and less spotted than an adult leopard.
- When the female leopard goes hunting, baby leopards wait in a cave or in rocky terrains. Babies hunt with their mothers when they are a couple months old.
- They live 7 to 10 years.

UPSIDE—DOWN BAOBAB
Figen Gündüz Letaconnoux

Once upon a time in West Africa, there was a huge tree called Baobab…in fact she was the first tree, and also creator of the other trees in the whole wide world.

As time passed, Baobab started having a strange feeling as she kept thinking that her siblings were better looking than her. She had never felt this strange new feeling before. As it kept growing it started to bother her… she even tried to find a name for it but she couldn't!

When Baobab saw how Palm Tree grew to be so tall, she wished to be as tall as he was, and even cried for it. She even wanted to grow the red glamorous flowers of Delonix Regia and also wanted to grow tasteful fruits like Fig.

Mother Nature was getting angry as she kept hearing Baobab's endless wishes, and decided to teach her a lesson…she took Baobab out of the ground and planted her upside-down!

After awhile, Mother Nature called on Baobab hoping that Baobab had learned her lesson and realized that her endless wishes were nonsense. Baobab was ashamed as she understood her mistake.

Mother Nature said "You are the ancestor of all trees; you should set an example for your siblings. Tell me…you were looking for a name for that feeling of yours, did you ever find one?"

Baobab answered, bowing her head; "No, I couldn't…"

Mother Nature told her that it was understandable why Baobab couldn't find a name for her feeling because it was a new feeling on earth and no one had ever felt it before. "It's called jealousy and I forbid everyone to feel it from now on!" Said Mother Nature. She continued "you didn't appreciate what you had. Instead of setting an example for your siblings, you were overwhelmed with this feeling… you need to pull yourself together!"

When Baobab left she started thinking about what she could do to see her good sides, as well as her bad sides. She then decided to make a list. She wrote "Good Sides" on one side of the list, and "Bad Sides" on the other. She then started writing her good sides…

- I am the oldest and the wisest tree in the world; my siblings listen and respect my opinions.
- I live for thousands of years and I can paint the nature green for 3 months a year.
- I can store almost 32,000 gallons of water during the rainy seasons. I don't need any water when it's hot, and my shell is always moist so fire can't affect me.
- My fruit, called "monkey bread," is full of vitamin C and is an important nutritional source for African people.
- People in Africa also make medicine with my fruit and leaves.
- People in the Western Region of Africa, especially in Angola, make delicious soup out of my fresh leaves and roots.
- I am a valuable addition to the African economy as people can make ropes with my fibers, and soap, fruit juice, dye and oil with my leaves.
- I hear lots of good news about how important I am for the African economy!

When Baobab was finished with her Good Sides, she started thinking about what she could write on the Bad Sides. She thought long and hard but couldn't really find anything bad to write. Then she came to a conclusion that she was just a good tree who helped every body, whether rich or poor.

She believed that her beautiful appearance was the reflection of her beautiful heart, and the important thing was the way she lived and how people would remember her.

Since that day she never lost her self-confidence, and never felt jealous again!

I was born in Istanbul, Turkey. I love nature, animals and kids.

For nearly 10 years, between 2006 and 2016, I've traveled to the least explored regions of the beautiful African Continent. I kept my camera with me at all times and took pictures of the unique beauty of Africa as I wrote my memoirs.

I have published two books of my memoirs, as well as photo journals for people who love to travel and explore. In addition to all this, I work on decal wood prints in my studio.

Since the very beginning, I've been writing and taking photos for *Atlas Çocuk Magazine* (a children's magazine in Turkey) about African nature, animals, and the lives of the African people.

For this book I've written stories of my own and also included local folktales from Africa to share with your kids.

Enjoy,
Figen Gündüz Letaconnoux

Other Books by Figen Gündüz Letaconnoux

Yaşamımdan Süzülen Afrika / Siyah İnci Yayınları, *October 2013*

İnsanlığın Beşiğine Yolculuk / Oğlak Yayınları, *April 2016*

In the immense African Continent, there are lots of cute animals living all together…

Stories are told about the African animals living happily together for ages. The stories I gathered, as well as the ones I wrote, are about African nature and animals.

Here, you will read about Baobab's virtue, the friendship between Warthog and Giraffe, how Giraffe got a long neck, Leopard's glamorous spots, and more.

Do you wonder about the interesting lives of African animals and want to learn real facts about those animals? I can hear you saying, "Yes!"

So let's start reading the stories…